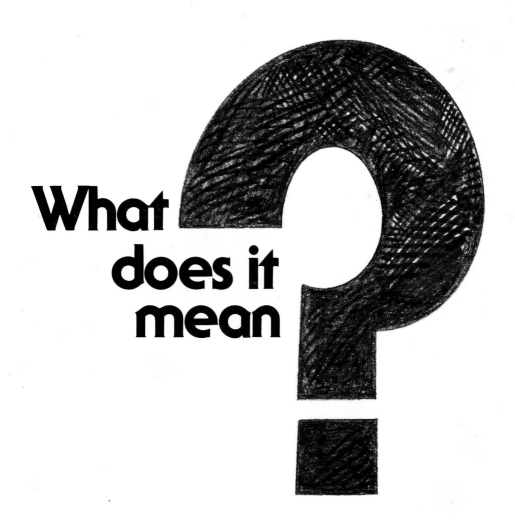

What does it mean ?

What does it mean?

SHARING

by Susan Riley

THE CHILD'S WORLD

ELGIN, ILLINOIS 60120

Art prepared by Collateral, Inc.

Distributed by Childrens Press, 1224 West Van Buren Street, Chicago, Illinois 60607.

Library of Congress Cataloging in Publication Data

Riley, Sue, 1946-
  Sharing.

  (What does it mean?)
  SUMMARY: Delineates things one can share and the effects of sharing.
  1. Sharing—Juvenile literature. [1. Sharing.
2] Conduct of life. I. Title.
BF575.S48R54   170'.202'22   77-16293
ISBN 0-89565-015-0

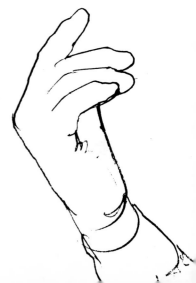

Hi, hello. Yes, it is me.

I'm here to share
with you, you'll see.
Sharing is something
all of us can do.

It means, "Some for me and some for you."

You can share almost
anything, anything at all.

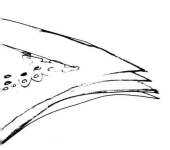

You can share a book,

an apple
or a
big beach ball.

Sharing your things shows
you are kind. Sharing says,

"You can play too;
I don't mind."

If you . . .

hear a joke
or even a riddle,
share it with others
and make everyone giggle.

Some things just
have to be shared__
yes, they do,
such as hugs
and kisses

and handshakes, too.

If you're feeling unhappy
or just feeling sad,

sharing your sadness
helps you feel glad.

I like to share.
And I share quite a lot.
You can share, too.
You can share what
you've got.

To show that you
love someone,
to show that you care,

just take
someone's
hand
and
say,
"Come, let's
share."

Books in this series

170
R   Riley, Susan

        What does it mean?
        Sharing

$10.

Rm 38

170
R   Riley, Susan

        What does it mean?
          Sharing

$10.60

DATE	BORROWER'S NAME	
2/2/92	Erica	14
11/1/92	Jeff	
1993	Tavares	38